Fun Fan Facts:

The Unofficial NBA Edition

Detroit Pistons

Everything Young Pistons Fans Should Know

By: Jake Liam

Dedication

To the city of Detroit. You built the cars that built America, survived things that would have broken most cities, and somehow produced one of the toughest basketball teams in history along the way.

And to every kid who has ever been told they are too small, too slow, or not talented enough to compete. Isiah Thomas was 6 feet 1 inch and ran the whole show. Ben Wallace went undrafted and won four Defensive Player of the Year awards. The Pistons never had the biggest names. They just had the biggest hearts. This one is for the underdogs who refuse to stay that way.

Detroit knows exactly who you are.

THE NBA BY THE NUMBERS

MOST NBA CHAMPIONSHIPS[*]

- CELTICS (18)
- LAKERS (17)
- WARRIORS (7)
- BULLS (6)
- SPURS (5)

As of the 2024-25 Season. † One Trophy = 4 Championships.

NBA HISTORY SNAPSHOT

1946 NBA Founded

1954 Shot Clock Introduced

1979 3-Point Line Added

2023 NBA Cup Introduced

BIG NUMBERS

$156 million
Stephen Curry's est. earnings in the 24-25 season

7'7"
Tallest player in NBA history (Gheorghe Mureșan & Manute Bol)

30 — 4 — 82

30 Teams Competing in the NBA

4 Playoff Rounds

82 Games Per Season

DETROIT PISTONS
IN THE NBA

- FOUNDED: 1941 [†]
- NBA TITLES: 3
- CONFERENCE TITLES: 4[*]

6 Consecutive Conference Finals (2003-2008)

*† Founding dates are complicated & may cause arguments at Thanksgiving. Ask someone born before color TV. All Titles reflect pre-relocation franchise history. * As of 2024-25 Season.*

NBA ALL-TIME MVP LEADERS

KAREEM ABDUL-JABBAR (6) ★ MICHAEL JORDAN (5) ★ BILL RUSSELL (5)

EASTERN CONFERENCE

- Atlantic – **Celtics**
- Atlantic – **Nets**
- Atlantic – **Knicks**
- Atlantic – **76ers**
- Atlantic – **Raptors**
- Central – **Bulls**
- Central – **Cavaliers**
- Central – **Pistons**
- Central – **Pacers**
- Central – **Bucks**
- Southeast – **Hawks**
- Southeast – **Hornets**
- Southeast – **Heat**
- Southeast – **Magic**
- Southeast – **Wizards**

WESTERN CONFERENCE

- Pacific – **Lakers**
- Pacific – **Clippers**
- Pacific – **Warriors**
- Pacific – **Suns**
- Pacific – **Kings**
- Northwest – **Nuggets**
- Northwest – **Timberwolves**
- Northwest – **Thunder**
- Northwest – **Trail Blazers**
- Northwest – **Jazz**
- Southwest – **Mavericks**
- Southwest – **Rockets**
- Southwest – **Spurs**
- Southwest – **Pelicans**
- Southwest – **Grizzlies**

Introduction

Welcome, fans! Whether you're new to cheering for the Detroit Pistons or you've been bleeding the team colors your whole life, this book is packed with fun, exciting facts about your favorite team. Get ready to impress your friends and family with everything you know about the Pistons.

Quick Time Out

This book is packed with stats. Like, A LOT of stats. Every fact was checked, double-checked, and triple-checked. But here's the thing about basketball history: not everyone agrees on everything. Ask someone who watched games before color TV and someone who grew up with instant replay and you'll get two completely different answers. My dad, stepdad, uncle, and grandpa all argued about the same fact. Four people. Four answers. All of them think they're right. So if you spot something that doesn't match what you've heard, congratulations. You might be a bigger fan than the people who helped make this book. And honestly? That's pretty cool.

HOW IT WORKS

THE SEASON
82 Games. One Goal.
Each team plays 82 games.
Win enough to make the
Playoffs.
Every game counts!
PLAYOFFS
30 Teams. 16 Make It.
8 per conference make the playoffs.
Win=Advance | Lose=Go Home
Best record
gets home court!
PLAYOFF ROUNDS
Best of 7. Win 4 or Go Home.
4 rounds of pure pressure.
Every series is do-or-die!
OVERTIME?
5 More Minutes.
Keep playing until
someone pulls ahead.
No ties. Ever.
THE FINALS
One Series. One Champion.
Winner lifts the Trophy.
Legend status unlocked.

How the NBA Works

At first glance, basketball feels simple. Ten players. One ball. Two hoops. Go.

Then the NBA adds the layers.

An 82-game regular season. A draft where bad teams pick first. Playoffs that last two full months. Superstars who can change everything with one trade. Dynasties that rise, fall, and rise again.

And somehow, it all works.

The NBA is built on one big idea: every team gets a chance to reset, reload, and rise again. No relegation. No dropping down to a lower league. Just basketball, every night, from October through June.

It is a league designed for drama, stars, and comebacks. And once you understand the flow, it is impossible to stop watching.

The League Setup

The NBA has 30 teams, spread across the United States and Canada. Those teams are split into two conferences:

- Eastern Conference
- Western Conference

Each conference has three divisions, mostly based on geography. Divisions matter for scheduling, but not as much as they used to.

Every team plays 82 regular season games, usually from October through April. Home games. Road games. Back-to-back nights. Long road trips. The season is a marathon before the sprint even starts.

Win games, and you climb the standings. Lose too many, and the pressure builds fast.

How Games Are Played

An NBA game has four quarters, each lasting 12 minutes. That means 48 minutes of game time, plus timeouts, free throws, and the occasional coach argument that adds another 20 minutes nobody planned for.

Scoring is simple:

- A shot inside the three-point line is worth 2 points
- A shot beyond the arc is worth 3 points
- Free throws are worth 1 point

If the score is tied at the end of regulation, the game goes to overtime, which lasts 5 minutes. Still tied? Another overtime. Keep going until someone wins.

There is a shot clock too. Teams have 24 seconds to take a shot. No standing around. No holding the ball forever. Keep it moving.

The Regular Season Race

The regular season is long for a reason. It tests everything.

Depth. Health. Focus. Patience.

Teams play opponents from both conferences, but they face conference rivals more often. By the end of the season, each conference's top teams have earned their playoff spots the hard way.

The goal is simple: make the playoffs. But there is a twist.

The NBA Cup

In 2023, the NBA added something new to the middle of the season. Something with actual stakes. They called it the In-Season Tournament, now known as the NBA Cup.

It works like this: Every team plays a small group stage during November and December, with special court designs that look like nothing else in basketball. The best teams advance to a knockout round held in Las Vegas.

The winners split a prize pool. Players earn bonus money. And for the first time, a team could lift a trophy before the playoffs even started.

Some fans are still warming up to it. Some players love it. But the moment a team starts treating it seriously and a crowd shows up buzzing in December, it feels like something.

Which, honestly, sounds about right.

The Play-In Tournament

Instead of sending the top eight teams from each conference straight to the playoffs, the NBA added something new. The Play-In Tournament.

Here is how it works:

- Teams ranked 1 through 6 in each conference are safe
- Teams ranked 7 through 10 fight for the final two playoff spots

The 7 and 8 seeds have an advantage. Win once and you are in. Lose and you still get one more shot. The 9 and 10 seeds have to win twice in a row just to earn a first-round matchup.

It turns the end of the season into a sprint. Every game suddenly matters more. Fans love it. Coaches age rapidly.

The NBA Playoffs

Once the playoffs begin, everything tightens.

Sixteen teams enter. Eight from each conference. Every round is a best-of-seven games series. That means the first team to win four games moves on:

- First Round
- Conference Semifinals
- Conference Finals
- NBA Finals

Home-court advantage matters. Crowds get louder. Rotations get shorter. Superstars play heavier minutes. One bad quarter can flip a series. One great performance can define a career.

By the time the NBA Finals arrive in June, only two teams are left. One from the East. One from the West. Four wins away from a championship. Four wins away from history.

The NBA Draft: Hope Begins Here

Here is where the NBA gets clever. Every summer, new players enter the league through the NBA Draft. Teams take turns selecting college players, international stars, and teenagers straight out of high school.

The teams that finished with the worst records get the best odds to pick early through the Draft Lottery. It is not guaranteed, but it gives struggling franchises a real shot at changing their future with one pick.

That means one bad season does not doom you forever. It might actually change everything. Some franchises are rebuilt by a single draft night moment.

Hope shows up wearing a new jersey.

No Relegation. All Pressure.

Unlike many global sports leagues, NBA teams never drop down to a lower league. They always stay in the NBA.

That does not mean there is no pressure.

Fans remember losing seasons. Owners make changes. Coaches get replaced. Players get traded. Every year is a test of direction, patience, and belief.

Stars, Systems, and Showtime

The NBA is famous for its stars. But stars do not win alone.

Teams need chemistry. Coaches need systems. Role players need to deliver on the biggest stages. One injury. One hot streak. One trade deadline deal. Any of it can flip a season.

That balance between individual brilliance and team basketball is what makes the league special.

Fast breaks. Buzzer-beaters. Game 7s. And moments that get replayed forever. That is the NBA.

Once you get the flow, it is pure electricity.

Detroit Pistons Facts

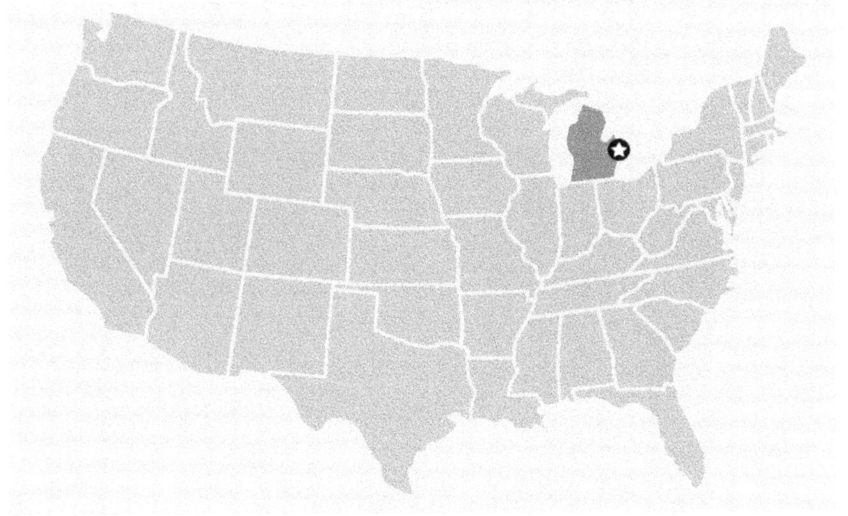

Home City

Detroit, Michigan

Metro Area Population

About 4.4 Million

Home Arena

Little Caesars Arena

Arena Capacity

20,332

Conference / Division

Eastern Conference / Central Division

Famous Local Food

Coney Island Hot Dogs, Detroit-Style Square Pizza,
Better Made Chips

Chapter 1: Motor City Origins

1. Not From Detroit: The Fort Wayne Zollner Pistons

The Detroit Pistons are one of the toughest, most physical, most relentless teams in NBA history. Physical. Gritty. Built like the city they represent. There is just one small problem with that origin story: they are not actually from Detroit.

Before they were the Detroit Pistons, they were the Fort Wayne Zollner Pistons, named after Fred Zollner, the man who owned them and paid for everything. Zollner ran a piston manufacturing company in Fort Wayne, Indiana. In 1941 he decided to fund a basketball team the same way other rich guys bought yachts. Except his yacht could box out, set screens, and win back-to-back NBL championships in 1944 and 1945. Fort Wayne, Indiana. Not exactly the center of the basketball universe. But Zollner was serious, the team was good, and they kept winning long enough to eventually join the NBA when it formed and make the Finals in 1955 and 1956.

By 1957, Zollner looked at his small-market team, looked at the booming city of Detroit two states over, and made a decision. Fort Wayne got a very polite goodbye. Detroit got a basketball team. And somewhere in Fort Wayne, Indiana, there is probably still a guy who has never fully gotten over it.

2. Why "Pistons": Thank the Assembly Line

When the team relocated to Detroit in 1957, they could have changed the name. Lots of teams do that. Start fresh, new city, new identity. But the Pistons kept their name, and in Detroit, that name landed differently. It did not just sound like a basketball team anymore. It sounded like the city itself.

Detroit was the automobile capital of the world. Ford, General Motors, and Chrysler all called it home. The city's entire economy ran on manufacturing, and the piston was one of the most essential parts of any engine. It moves up and down inside the cylinder, converting fuel into power, turning explosions into motion. Without pistons, cars don't go anywhere.

So when Detroit fans looked at their new basketball team and saw the name "Pistons," it clicked. These were not just basketball players. They were part of the machine. Hard-working, mechanical, built to keep moving no matter what. Decades later, when the Bad

Boys teams started throwing elbows and winning championships through sheer toughness, that name felt like destiny. A piston does not finesse you. It just keeps driving forward until something breaks. Usually whatever is in the way.

3. The Struggling Sixties: Growing Pains in the Motor City

The early years in Detroit were not exactly a highlight reel. The Pistons spent most of the 1960s stuck in that uncomfortable place that is not quite bad enough to get top draft picks but not quite good enough to go anywhere in the playoffs. They made the postseason a few times. They lost early. They went home. They tried again.

What they did have was Dave Bing, one of the most gifted players the franchise ever saw, and we will get to him in a later chapter. But around Bing, the roster was inconsistent. Coaches came and went. Strategies changed. The team was searching for an identity the way you search for your phone in the morning: a little desperate, a little confused, and not entirely sure it is going to turn up.

Imagine sitting in Cobo Arena in 1965, watching your team lose another close one, wondering if this franchise would ever figure it out. Fans stayed loyal anyway, because Detroit fans are built that way. The patience they showed during those early years was the same patience they would need decades later during another long rebuild. Some things about this franchise never change. Good thing patience is one of them.

4. Playing in a Football Stadium: The Silverdome Years

In 1978, the Pistons made a move that sounds completely insane when you say it out loud: they decided to play basketball in a stadium built for football. The Pontiac Silverdome, located in the Detroit suburb of Pontiac, had a capacity of over 80,000 people for football. For basketball, they reconfigured it to hold around 22,000. That sounds fine until you realize the atmosphere of a 22,000-person crowd inside an 80,000-seat dome feels approximately like playing in an airport hangar during a thunderstorm.

The sightlines were bad. The floor sat in the middle of a space designed for something completely different. It was loud in all the wrong ways and quiet in all the wrong places. Players and fans generally agreed it was not ideal. What it was, though, was big. On special occasions, the Pistons actually used that size. In 1988, they set what was then the NBA attendance record with over 61,000 fans packed in for a playoff game against the Boston Celtics.

Sixty-one thousand people watching a basketball game. That is not a basketball crowd. That is a small country. The Pistons lost that game, by the way. But nobody forgot it.

5. The Palace of Auburn Hills: A Home Worth Having

In 1988, the Pistons opened what would become one of the most celebrated arenas in NBA history: The Palace of Auburn Hills. And the timing could not have been more perfect, because the team that moved in was about to become one of the most feared teams in NBA history.

The Palace was privately funded, which was unusual for that era. Owner Bill Davidson paid for it himself without asking the public for money. The building seated just over 22,000 fans and was designed specifically for basketball, which after the Silverdome felt like moving from a tent into a mansion. Great sightlines. Loud acoustics. A crowd that sat close enough to make visiting players genuinely uncomfortable.

The Pistons won two championships in their new home in 1989 and 1990. They went back to the Finals in 2004 and won again. For opposing teams, a road game at the Palace was considered one of the toughest tests in the league. The crowd was loud, knowledgeable, and completely unforgiving. The Palace closed in 2017 when the team moved to Little Caesars Arena in downtown Detroit. It was demolished in 2020. But if you ask any Pistons fan of a certain age about that building, watch their face. That is not nostalgia. That is pride.

6. Isiah Thomas: The Little General (1981-1994)

Isiah Thomas was listed at 6 feet 1 inch tall, which is a perfectly reasonable height for a human being and a completely unreasonable height for a player trying to run an NBA team full of giants. He did it anyway, and he did it better than almost anyone who has ever played the position.

Thomas was drafted second overall by Detroit in 1981 out of Indiana University, where he had just won a national championship as a freshman. He was quick in ways that made defenders look like they were moving through wet cement. He could get to the basket, pull up for the mid-range jumper, or find an open teammate before the defense even registered what was happening. In thirteen seasons with the Pistons, he averaged 19.2 points and 9.3 assists per game. Numbers like those are the mark of a truly elite point guard. He was a twelve-time All-Star. He won two championship rings. He finished his career as one of the most accomplished point guards in the history of the sport.

But what set Thomas apart was not the stats. It was the will. He was the engine of those Bad Boys teams, the player opponents focused on stopping first and the player who found a way to score anyway. In Game 6 of the 1988 Finals, he scored 25 points in a single quarter on a badly sprained ankle, hobbling up and down the court and still finding ways to hurt the Lakers. The Pistons lost that game, but nobody forgot what they watched. That quarter alone is enough to build a legend on.

Isiah Thomas pushes the ball up the court for the Detroit Pistons during a 1985 game against the New York Knicks at Madison Square Garden. Quick handles. Sharp vision. The floor general running the show. *Photo: "Isiah Thomas, Detroit vs. New York (1985)" by Rick Dikeman. Licensed under CC BY-SA 2.0. Source: Wikimedia Commons.*

7. Dennis Rodman: The Rebounding Alien (1986-1993)

Dennis Rodman did not play basketball the way other people play basketball. He played it the way a scientist might study it, obsessing over angles, trajectories, and patterns until he understood exactly where the ball was going before it got there. He was listed at 6 feet 7 inches, which made him a small forward, except he led the league in rebounding seven straight seasons and outrebounded players four inches taller than him on a nightly basis.

Rodman grew up in Dallas, Texas, in difficult circumstances, and did not start playing organized basketball until his late teens. He went to a small NAIA college and was not exactly a highly touted recruit. The Pistons took him in the second round of the 1986 draft, which means they got one of the greatest rebounders in history for next to nothing. He was relentless on the boards, throwing his body around with zero concern for personal safety. He would dive on the floor, crash through crowds, and fight for every single possession as if the fate of the world depended on which team got the ball.

Off the court, Rodman became one of the most colorful personalities in sports history, with the dyed hair and the reality TV appearances and the whole Dennis Rodman Experience that most people know from later in his career. But in Detroit, he was something purer: a teammate who outworked everyone and asked for nothing except the chance to do it again tomorrow. He won two championships as a Piston and is in the Hall of Fame. Not bad for a second-round pick nobody was sure about.

8. Bill Laimbeer: The Guy Every Other Team Hated (1982-1994)

There is a specific category of NBA player that every championship team needs and almost no one will admit to liking: the enforcer. The guy who sets screens that leave bruises. The guy who fouls hard enough that you think about it the next day. The guy who trash-talks during free throws and somehow gets under your skin even when you are thirty points ahead. Bill Laimbeer was all of that, and he was great at it.

Laimbeer played center for the Pistons for twelve seasons and was one of the most disliked players in the league by everyone who did not play alongside him. Opponents hated his physical style, his flagrant fouls, and the way he never seemed to feel bad about any of it. His teammates loved him for exactly the same reasons. He was the guy who made the Bad Boys feel genuinely dangerous.

What people forget about Laimbeer is that he could actually play. He was not just a bruiser. He had a reliable mid-range shot and was a skilled rebounder who averaged over nine boards per game for his career. He was a four-time All-Star, which is something people never bring up when they are busy complaining about his elbows. He won two championships, retired, and then became one of the most successful coaches in WNBA history, winning four titles with the Detroit Shock and Las Vegas Aces. Turns out all that knowledge about how to win translated pretty well when he switched to the other side of the clipboard.

9. Chauncey Billups: Mr. Big Shot (2002-2008, 2010-2011)

Chauncey Billups had a nickname that tells you everything: Mr. Big Shot. Not because someone handed it to him. Because he kept making enormous shots in enormous moments until there was no other name that fit.

Billups was drafted by Boston in 1997 and spent years bouncing around the league, playing for five different teams in his first five seasons. He was talented but could not seem to find the right situation. Then Detroit took a chance on him in 2002, and something clicked. The Pistons needed a calm, intelligent point guard who could lead a team built around defense and toughness. Billups turned out to be exactly that person, which is either great scouting or extraordinary luck, and probably some of both.

He was the glue of the 2004 championship team, the player who made everyone around him better and stepped up every single time the lights got brightest. He won Finals MVP in 2004 after averaging 21 points per game in the series against the Los Angeles Lakers, a team that most of the basketball world expected to win in four games. He made the tough shot. He made the free throw. He made the decision. Over and over, in five games, until the Pistons were champions and Billups was the reason. That kind of reliable ice-cold clutch performance is the rarest thing in basketball. Not everyone can manufacture it on demand. Billups made it look like breathing.

10. Ben Wallace: Too Big to Ignore, Too Tough to Stop (2000-2006, 2009-2012)

Here is the most remarkable fact about Ben Wallace: no team in the entire NBA wanted to draft him. Not one. He went undrafted in 1996, which means every single franchise looked at him and said "no thank you" and moved on. The Pistons eventually signed him four years later, in 2000, and watched him become the most dominant defensive player in the league.

Wallace stood 6 feet 9 inches with a wingspan and physical strength that made him seem larger. He wore an enormous afro that became one of the most recognizable looks in the sport. And he played defense at a level that genuinely changed how opponents approached their offense. He won four Defensive Player of the Year awards, which is tied for the most in NBA history. He made four All-Star teams. He averaged over ten rebounds per game for most of his career in Detroit.

What he could not do was shoot. His career free throw percentage was around 41 percent, which is genuinely one of the lowest in NBA history for a regular starter. Opposing coaches sometimes had their players intentionally foul Wallace just to put him on the line, a strategy called Hack-a-Shaq that became Hack-a-Ben. None of that stopped him. He just went and got the rebound on his own miss, because of course he did. The guy nobody wanted ended up being the kind of player championship teams are built around. Every team that passed on him in 1996 had to watch him hold up a trophy in 2004. That is either a very funny story or a very painful one, depending on which team you work for.

- 29 -

Chapter 3: Fights, Finals, and Upsets

11. Sweeping the Lakers: The 1989 Championship

The 1989 NBA Finals matched the Detroit Pistons against the Los Angeles Lakers, and most of the basketball world expected a close, competitive series. The Lakers had Magic Johnson. They had a dynasty. They had won five championships that decade. The Pistons had Bill Laimbeer, Isiah Thomas on a bad ankle, and an absolute refusal to be impressed by any of it.

Detroit swept Los Angeles four games to zero. Not four-one. Not four-two. Four and zero. The Lakers never won a single game. Magic Johnson left the series early with a hamstring injury, but the honest truth is that Detroit had already taken the soul out of that team before anyone got hurt. The Pistons held LA under 100 points in every single game. They smothered. They grabbed. They pushed. They made beautiful Showtime Lakers basketball look like a Tuesday afternoon on the 405.

Isiah Thomas was named Finals MVP after averaging 27.6 points per game on a sprained ankle that would have had most players sitting in street clothes on the bench. The Pistons celebrated on the court at the Forum in Los Angeles, in enemy territory, which made it exactly twice as satisfying. Detroit had its first championship. The Bad Boys had arrived. And the Lakers needed a very long nap.

12. Back to Back: Detroit Does It Again in 1990

Winning one championship is hard. Winning two in a row is one of the rarest things in professional sports, because after you win, everyone spends an entire year studying exactly how you did it and building a specific plan to stop you. The Pistons didn't care. They came back in 1990 and did it again.

The 1990 Finals sent Detroit against the Portland Trail Blazers, a talented team with Clyde Drexler leading the charge. The Pistons won in five games. Isiah Thomas won his second Finals MVP. The defense was every bit as suffocating as it had been the year before. The Bad Boys were not a one-year story. They were a dynasty, a short and extremely violent one, but a dynasty.

What made the back-to-back especially meaningful was the team that Detroit had to go through to get there. In the Eastern Conference Finals, they eliminated the Chicago Bulls in seven games. Michael Jordan was already one of the best players on the planet. The Pistons stopped him anyway, using their infamous Jordan Rules defensive system, because they had a specific answer for every question Jordan asked. Two championships. Two years. One identity. Detroit was not lucky. Detroit was just better.

13. The Upset Nobody Saw Coming: The 2004 Championship

By 2004, the Los Angeles Lakers had assembled what many people considered a guaranteed championship roster. Shaquille O'Neal, the most dominant center in the game. Kobe Bryant, one of the best scorers alive. Karl Malone and Gary Payton, two future Hall of Famers added specifically to fill in the gaps. Las Vegas oddsmakers installed them as massive favorites. Television analysts picked them in five games. Some picked them in four. It was basically a coronation waiting to happen.

Nobody told the Pistons.

Detroit beat Los Angeles in five games. The same five games everyone predicted for the Lakers, except the Pistons won them. Chauncey Billups was Finals MVP. Rasheed Wallace was everywhere. Ben Wallace muscled Shaquille O'Neal around in ways that seemed physically improbable. The Pistons had no single superstar. They had five guys who played their roles perfectly, trusted each other completely, and guarded with a ferocity that the Lakers never found an answer for. It is still considered one of the biggest upsets in Finals history. Somewhere, every analyst who predicted a Lakers sweep in four still does not love thinking about it.

14. The Malice at the Palace: The Night Everything Changed

On November 19, 2004, the Detroit Pistons hosted the Indiana Pacers at the Palace of Auburn Hills. With 45 seconds left and the game mostly decided, Ron Artest of Indiana fouled Ben Wallace hard near the basket. Wallace shoved back. Players came off the benches. It looked like a standard NBA scuffle that would result in some technical fouls and a lot of serious-looking conversations.

Then a cup of Diet Coke flew out of the stands and hit Artest in the chest. And everything went sideways in a direction nobody had ever seen before.

Artest went into the stands. Teammates followed. Fans threw things. Players threw things back. The game was stopped with 45 seconds remaining and never resumed. Nine players were suspended, with Artest receiving a then-record 86-game ban that cost him essentially the entire season. It was the most serious on-court incident in modern NBA history and triggered immediate rule changes about player-fan interactions, court access, and security protocols. The NBA put up higher scorer's table barriers at every arena. The way players and fans interact was never quite the same again. One cup of soda, 45 seconds left, and an entire sport had to look at itself and figure out what had just happened.

15. Grant Hill: The Future That Almost Was

When Grant Hill arrived as the third overall pick in the 1994 draft, the Pistons believed they had found the player who would carry them into their next era. And for a few years, that looked exactly right. Hill was exceptional. Smooth, athletic, capable of scoring, passing, and defending at a level that put him in conversations with the best players in the league. He shared Rookie of the Year honors in his first season. He made six All-Star teams. He was the kind of player who made the game look easy because he had already done all the hard work before the ball left his hands.

Then the injuries came. Ankle problems that started small and grew into something serious. Surgeries. Recoveries that did not stick. More surgeries. By 2000, Hill left Detroit for Orlando in free agency, chasing a fresh start and a chance to put the injuries behind him. It did not go the way anyone hoped.

But here is what Grant Hill's Detroit years actually gave the franchise: proof that it could attract a legitimate star. The Pistons had been built on toughness and grit since Fort Wayne, and Hill represented something different, a glimpse of a future where Detroit could have both. He never delivered a championship in

Detroit, but he delivered six years of basketball that reminded the city what genuine talent looked like. Sometimes the bridge to what is next is the most important piece, even when it does not feel that way at the time.

Chapter 4: Detroit Grit: Traditions, Nicknames, and the Bad Boy Identity

16. The Bad Boys: Where the Name Came From

The nickname did not come from a committee. It did not come from a marketing meeting or a focus group or someone in the front office trying to build a brand. It came from the way the team played, and it stuck because it was the most accurate two words anyone could find.

The Pistons of the late 1980s were physical in ways that made opponents genuinely unhappy. They fouled hard. They talked trash. They played defense like they had a personal grudge against every player they were guarding. Rick Mahorn and Bill Laimbeer hit people. Dennis Rodman annoyed people. Isiah Thomas outscored people and then smiled about it while the other team was still trying to figure out what happened. The whole roster had an edge.

Reporters and fans started calling them the Bad Boys almost organically, and the team leaned into it completely. They wore it like a badge. Detroit, a city that had been through economic collapse and was still fighting its way back, connected with it immediately. Their basketball team was not pretty. It was not elegant. It was effective and hard and it won championships. For a city that had spent decades hearing what it could not do, watching those Pistons teams do whatever they wanted to whoever they wanted felt exactly right.

17. The Jordan Rules: A Defensive Blueprint for Stopping the Unstoppable

Michael Jordan was the best player in basketball for most of the late 1980s. He could score from anywhere, finish through contact, and take over a game so completely that opponents sometimes just ran out of ideas. Most teams watched him go for 40 points and shrugged. The Pistons wrote a manual.

The Jordan Rules were a specific defensive scheme designed and implemented by Detroit coach Chuck Daly. The basic idea was to make every inch Jordan covered as physically difficult as possible. When Jordan drove left, he got hit. When he drove right, he got hit. When he rose up for a jumper, there was a hand in his face and a body making the landing uncomfortable. The Pistons did not try to take Jordan completely out of the game because that was impossible. They tried to make him earn every single point at maximum physical cost, and then make the players around him beat them. For three straight years in the playoffs, it worked.

Jordan himself later said the Pistons were the team he hated losing to most, which is either a critique or the highest possible compliment depending on how you look at it. Eventually, Jordan got stronger, his teammates got better, and Chicago broke through in 1991. But the Jordan Rules were studied and borrowed and discussed for decades afterward. You could not stop the best player in the world. The Pistons at least made him tired while he was doing it.

18. Dave Bing: From Scoring Champion to Mayor of Detroit

Dave Bing was the Detroit Pistons' first great player, a Hall of Fame guard who led the entire NBA in scoring in just his second professional season and made seven All-Star teams during his career. That would be enough for most people. Bing was not most people.

After retiring from basketball in 1978, Bing founded Bing Steel, a steel manufacturing company in Detroit. He built it into one of the most successful minority-owned businesses in the country, eventually employing thousands of workers and expanding into multiple industries. He did not move to a warmer city and play golf. He stayed in Detroit and built something.

Then in 2009, he ran for Mayor of Detroit and won. A scoring champion who became a Hall of Famer who became a CEO who became the mayor of a major American city. Most athletes retire and open a restaurant. Dave Bing ran one of the largest cities in the United States. If you ever meet someone who tries to tell you basketball players do not do much after their careers end, the correct response is to bring up Dave Bing and then wait quietly while they reconsider their position.

19. Detroit Faithful: Why Pistons Fans Hit Different

There are loud fan bases and then there is Detroit. The Palace of Auburn Hills was considered one of the most hostile road environments in the NBA for most of its existence. Opposing players talked about it. Coaches game-planned for the noise. The crowd knew the game, knew the players, and had absolutely no patience for teams that came in thinking they were going to have a comfortable night.

Part of it is the city itself. Detroit fans have a direct, no-nonsense relationship with their sports teams that reflects the city's broader identity. No one in Detroit is particularly interested in pretending things are fine when they are not, and no one stays quiet when the team delivers something worth celebrating. The Bad Boys era created a generation of fans who were taught by those championship teams that toughness and effort are the baseline requirements, not bonus features.

Even during the long lean years after the 2004 championship, Pistons fans kept showing up. They booed what deserved to be booed. They cheered what deserved to be cheered. They waited with the specific impatience of a fan base that knows exactly what winning looks like because they have seen it. That is not a casual fan base. That is a city that takes its basketball personally.

20. The Teal Years: When Detroit Got Experimental

In 1996, the Pistons unveiled new uniforms that introduced teal as an alternate color. Teal. For a franchise whose entire identity was built on being tough and no-nonsense and physically intimidating. Teal.

It was the 1990s, and every team in every sport seemed to be adding teal somewhere. The Jacksonville Jaguars had teal. The Florida Marlins had teal. The San Jose Sharks had teal. It was the decade's official color of questionable decision-making. The Pistons went with a horse logo on the alternate jerseys, moving away from their traditional wordmark identity in favor of something that looked more like a team about to play a game of beach volleyball than a team that had won two championships by being aggressively unpleasant to be around.

The uniforms lasted a few years before the franchise course-corrected back toward red, white, and blue. The teal era is remembered now mostly as a historical curiosity, the kind of thing that gets brought up at trivia nights and generates extremely strong opinions from fans who lived through it. The Pistons eventually returned to a more traditional look, which is probably what everyone involved preferred. Some teams are built for teal. The Bad Boys franchise was not one of them.

Chapter 5: Present Day: Rebuilding in the Motor City

21. Little Caesars Arena: A New Home Downtown

In 2017, the Pistons left Auburn Hills and moved back into the city of Detroit for the first time since 1978. Little Caesars Arena sits in the District Detroit, a development area designed to anchor the city's ongoing downtown revival. It holds just over 20,000 fans for basketball and shares the building with the Detroit Red Wings, which means on any given week the same floor that hosts an NHL team gets converted for the NBA. The Zamboni and the ball rack live in the same building. That is either very efficient or very confusing, depending on who you ask.

The arena itself is modern, loud, and centrally located in a way the Palace never was. Getting there does not require a highway drive to the suburbs. It sits in the middle of the city, which matters to Detroit in ways that go beyond just basketball. The move was part of a broader push to bring people, investment, and energy back into a downtown that had spent decades fighting its way back from economic collapse. The Pistons coming home was symbolic. Little Caesars Arena giving

fans a genuinely great place to watch games was
practical. Detroit needed both.

22. The Long Rebuild: What Happened After 2004

After the 2004 championship, the Pistons stayed
competitive for several more seasons, reaching the
Eastern Conference Finals in 2005, 2006, and 2007.
Then the core aged out, the roster broke down, and
Detroit entered a rebuilding period that lasted longer
than anyone in the organization would have preferred.

The years between 2009 and 2021 were lean. The
Pistons made the playoffs occasionally but never
seriously threatened to go deep. Draft picks came and
went with mixed results. Coaching changes happened
with the kind of regularity that suggests nobody had
quite figured out the right answer. Blake Griffin arrived
in 2018 as a trade acquisition and showed flashes of his
old star power before injuries reduced his
effectiveness. Andre Drummond was a force on the
glass but the team around him never came together
properly. It was a long stretch of almost-but-not-quite,
which is the most frustrating place any sports franchise
can find itself.

What the Pistons did during those years was accumulate draft capital and develop young players, which is the correct way to rebuild even when it does not feel satisfying in the moment. By 2021 they had the first overall pick in the draft. They used it on a 6-foot-6 point guard from Oklahoma State who plays the game with uncommon calm and makes everyone around him better. His name is Cade Cunningham, and he changes the entire conversation.

23. Cade Cunningham: The Cornerstone

Cade Cunningham was the first overall pick in the 2021 NBA Draft, which is the basketball equivalent of getting first pick in every category simultaneously. Height. Skill. Basketball IQ. Vision. Scoring ability. He has all of it, and he plays with a maturity that most players take a decade to develop.

Cunningham is listed at 6 feet 6 inches, which is enormous for a point guard. He can see over defenders that smaller guards cannot, which changes what is possible in the pick and roll, the drive and kick, and basically every offensive action the Pistons want to run. He averaged over 22 points, 4 rebounds, and 6 assists per game in the 2023-24 season before injuries interrupted his year. When healthy, he is one of the best young players in the Eastern Conference.

What makes Cunningham particularly exciting for Detroit fans is what he represents beyond the stats. He is the kind of foundational piece that championship teams are built around. Not a rental. Not a reclamation project. A 23-year-old franchise centerpiece who chose to stay in Detroit when he signed his max contract extension. He did not ask out. He did not demand a trade to a bigger market. He is here, he is committed, and if the roster around him develops the way the front office believes it will, the Pistons could be a serious team again sooner than most people expect. Detroit has waited for this before. They are good at it.

24. Monty Williams and the New Blueprint

In 2023, the Pistons made the most expensive head coaching hire in NBA history, signing Monty Williams to a six-year, $78.5 million contract. That is not a typo. Seventy-eight point five million dollars for a coach, which is more than most players make and sent a very clear message: the Pistons are serious about doing this correctly.

Williams had previously coached the Phoenix Suns to the NBA Finals in 2021 and was widely considered one of the best coaches in the league. Bringing him to Detroit signaled that ownership was not interested in a slow, gradual rebuild. They wanted to accelerate. Pair an elite young cornerstone in Cunningham with an elite head coach who knows how to build winning cultures, add pieces around them, and see what happens.

The 2023-24 season was difficult, with injuries piling up and the young roster still finding its footing. The Pistons lost a lot of games, including a stretch that broke the NBA record for consecutive losses in a season. That is a painful record to set. But Monty Williams has been through difficult rebuilds before and understands that the losses in year one are not the story. The development happening underneath them is. The foundation is in place. The question is how fast everything built on top of it rises.

25. Detroit's Future: Why the Next Chapter Looks Real

Every rebuild has a moment where it stops looking like hope and starts looking like evidence. For the Pistons, that moment is arriving. The front office has assembled one of the youngest rosters in the league around Cade Cunningham, with players like Jalen Duren, a powerful young center who was already forcing his way into All-Star conversations, and Ausar Thompson, an athletic wing whose defensive potential is genuinely exciting.

Detroit has draft picks. It has cap flexibility. It has a coaching staff that knows how to win and a front office that has shown patience without losing urgency. These are the ingredients. The Pistons have been through this before, in Fort Wayne in the 1940s, in Detroit in the 1970s, in Auburn Hills in the late 1980s, and they know what the other side of a rebuild looks like. It looks like championships.

The city of Detroit has been told for decades what it cannot do and what it cannot have. The Pistons, at their best, have always been the answer to that. Not flashy. Not lucky. Just built right and ready to go. The Bad Boys proved it in 1989 and 1990. The five-man machine proved it in 2004. And somewhere in Little Caesars Arena, a 23-year-old point guard with a max contract and a very long memory is building the next proof. Detroit does not hurry. It just wins eventually. Bet against that at your own risk.

- 50 -

Bonus Trivia Quiz!

You think you are a true Pistons fan? Try this bonus quiz!

1. The Detroit Pistons were originally based in which city before moving to Detroit?

A) Indianapolis, Indiana
B) Fort Wayne, Indiana
C) Columbus, Ohio
D) Louisville, Kentucky

2. Fred Zollner named the team the "Pistons" because he owned what kind of company?

A) A car dealership
B) A tire manufacturing company
C) A piston manufacturing company
D) A steel factory

3. Which unusual venue did the Pistons play in from 1978 before the Palace opened?

A) Ford Field
B) Tiger Stadium
C) The Pontiac Silverdome
D) Cobo Arena

4. How many Defensive Player of the Year awards did Ben Wallace win as a Piston?

A) Two
B) Three
C) Four
D) Five

5. Isiah Thomas was listed at what height, making his dominance even more remarkable?

A) 5 feet 11 inches
B) 6 feet 1 inch
C) 6 feet 3 inches
D) 6 feet 4 inches

6. What was the result of the 1989 NBA Finals between Detroit and the Los Angeles Lakers?

A) Lakers won in six games
B) Pistons won in six games
C) Pistons swept the Lakers four games to zero
D) Pistons won in seven games

7. Who won Finals MVP when the Pistons beat the Lakers in 2004?

A) Ben Wallace
B) Rasheed Wallace
C) Richard Hamilton
D) Chauncey Billups

8. The Malice at the Palace in 2004 was triggered when what flew out of the stands?

A) A hot dog
B) A cup of Diet Coke
C) A basketball
D) A program

9. What is the name of Detroit's current home arena, opened in 2017?

A) Palace of Auburn Hills
B) Ford Field Arena
C) Little Caesars Arena
D) Motor City Center

10. Before coaching in Detroit, Monty Williams took which team to the NBA Finals in 2021?

A) Oklahoma City Thunder
B) New Orleans Pelicans
C) Phoenix Suns
D) Memphis Grizzlies

11. The "Jordan Rules" were a defensive strategy designed by which Pistons head coach?

A) Larry Brown
B) Chuck Daly
C) Flip Saunders
D) Rick Carlisle

12. Dennis Rodman led the NBA in rebounding for how many straight seasons?

A) Four
B) Five
C) Six
D) Seven

13. After his basketball career, Dave Bing became famous for doing what in Detroit?

A) Owning the Pistons
B) Coaching the team
C) Becoming Mayor of Detroit
D) Building Little Caesars Arena

14. Cade Cunningham was selected with which pick in the 2021 NBA Draft?

A) Second overall
B) Third overall
C) First overall
D) Fifth overall

15. Which alternate color did the Pistons controversially introduce in 1996 that fans still argue about today?

A) Purple
B) Orange
C) Teal
D) Gold

Super Fan Secret Challenge

Only a true Pistons fan will know this.

(No Answer Provided)

Bill Laimbeer won NBA championships as a player with the Detroit Pistons, then went on to become one of the most successful coaches in WNBA history. How many WNBA championships did Laimbeer win as a head coach, and which two franchises did he win them with?

Answer Key

1. B) Fort Wayne, Indiana

2. C) A piston manufacturing company

3. C) The Pontiac Silverdome

4. C) Four

5. B) 6 feet 1 inch

6. C) Pistons swept the Lakers four games to zero

7. D) Chauncey Billups

8. B) A cup of Diet Coke

9. C) Little Caesars Arena

10. C) Phoenix Suns

11. B) Chuck Daly

12. D) Seven

13. C) Becoming Mayor of Detroit

14. C) First overall

15. C) Teal

NBA PLAYOFF BRACKET

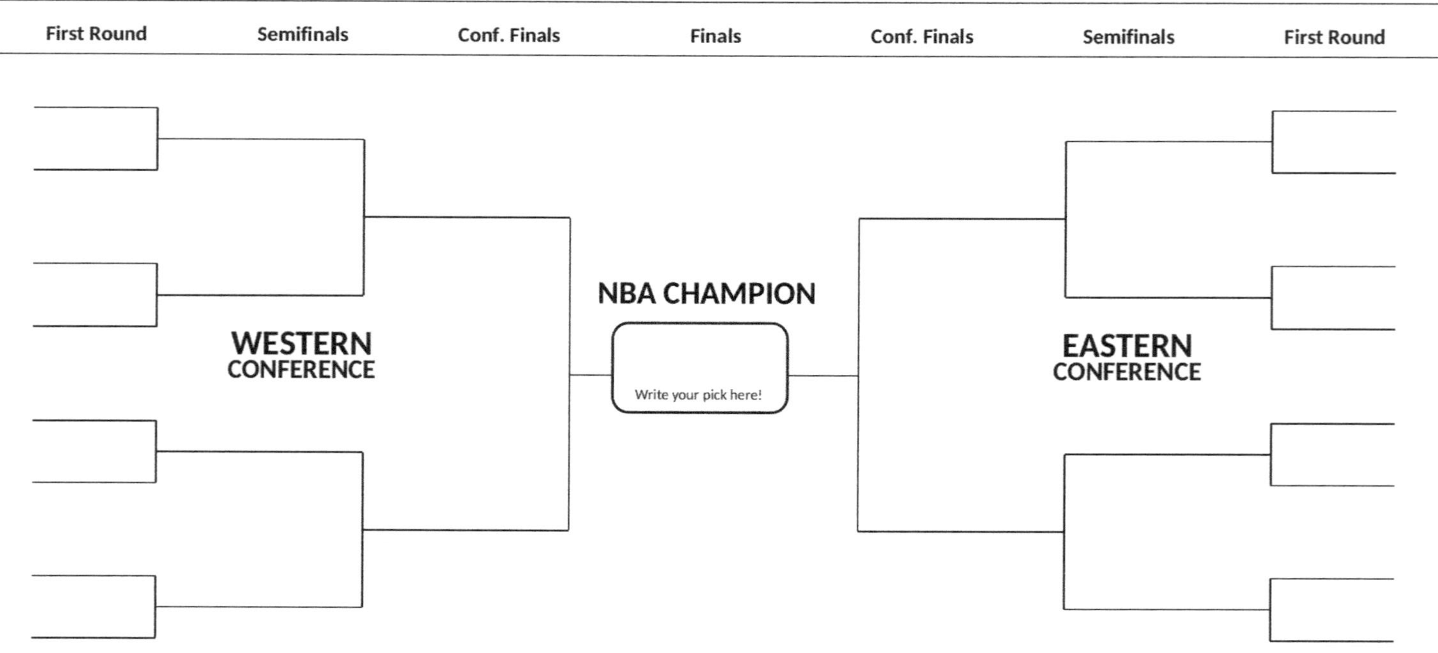

* Fill in your picks and try not to argue with your friends about it!

Part of the Fun Fan Facts: The Unofficial Sports Guide Series

Be the Boss of the Playoffs

You've broken down the matchups. You know which superstar takes over in the fourth quarter. You've seen the bench units that quietly decide series. You've watched the adjustments coaches make when their backs are against the wall.

Now it's time to stop watching and start deciding.

On this page, you are not just a fan. You are the Head Coach drawing up the last play with three seconds left on the clock. You are the GM who built this roster. You are the analyst who saw it all coming.

This is not just filling out a bracket.

This is building your championship run.

Sixteen teams enter the NBA Playoffs. The path is brutal. Best of seven. No shortcuts. No hiding. Every round gets louder, harder, and more personal.

This bracket is your Playoff Control Room.

The Game Plan

1. Survive Round One: Start with the opening round. Which matchup is going seven games? Who has the closer? Who folds under pressure? Make the calls.

2. Feel the Momentum: As you move into the Conference Semifinals and Conference Finals, things change. Role players become heroes. Stars feel the weight. Trust your reads.

3. Own the Finals: Trace your picks all the way to the NBA Finals. When the confetti falls and the trophy is raised, you'll find out who earned it.

House Rules: Circle your boldest upset. That is your official "I knew it" moment.

Choose Your Weapon: Pencil if you want flexibility. Pen if you trust your instincts. Sharpie if you believe in chaos.

Because once the playoffs tip off, there is no rewinding Game 7.

Make your picks. Trust your basketball brain. And let the playoff drama begin.

Fun Facts Wrap-Up

You made it through! You're officially a true superfan! Now it's time to put your knowledge to the test. Share these facts with friends and see who really knows their team best.

Love the series?

Your reviews help other fans discover Fun Fan Facts. If you enjoyed this book, we'd really appreciate you sharing your thoughts and leaving a review.

Want more Fun Fan Facts?

Scan the QR code below to visit our site and explore bonus trivia, challenges, and special extras - including new teams, future series, and collectible fun as they're released.

Collect All the Fun Fan Facts Series!

Check off every book you read. See the full set on Amazon. Search "Fun Fan Facts Jake Liam."

World Cup 2026 Edition

☐ Algeria
☐ France
☐ Paraguay
☐ Argentina
☐ Germany
☐ Portugal
☐ Australia
☐ Ghana
☐ Qatar
☐ Austria
☐ Haiti
☐ Saudi Arabia
☐ Belgium
☐ Iran

☐ Scotland
☐ Brazil
☐ Ivory Coast
☐ Senegal
☐ Canada
☐ Japan
☐ South Africa
☐ Cape Verde
☐ Jordan
☐ South Korea
☐ Colombia
☐ Mexico
☐ Spain
☐ Croatia

☐ Morocco
☐ Switzerland
☐ Curaçao
☐ Netherlands
☐ Tunisia
☐ Ecuador
☐ New Zealand
☐ United States
☐ Egypt
☐ Norway
☐ Uruguay
☐ England
☐ Panama
☐ Uzbekistan

World Cup 2026 Group Edition

☐ Group A
☐ Group E
☐ Group I
☐ Group B

☐ Group F
☐ Group J
☐ Group C
☐ Group G

☐ Group K
☐ Group D
☐ Group H
☐ Group L

English Football Edition

- ☐ Arsenal F.C.
- ☐ Aston Villa F.C.
- ☐ Chelsea F.C.
- ☐ Everton F.C.
- ☐ Fulham F.C.
- ☐ Liverpool F.C.
- ☐ Manchester City
- ☐ Manchester United
- ☐ Newcastle United F.C.
- ☐ Tottenham Hotspur
- ☐ West Ham United
- ☐ Wrexham A.F.C.

NBA Edition

- ☐ Atlanta Hawks
- ☐ Boston Celtics
- ☐ Brooklyn Nets
- ☐ Charlotte Hornets
- ☐ Chicago Bulls
- ☐ Cleveland Cavaliers
- ☐ Dallas Mavericks
- ☐ Denver Nuggets
- ☐ Detroit Pistons
- ☐ Golden State Warriors
- ☐ Houston Rockets
- ☐ Indiana Pacers
- ☐ LA Clippers
- ☐ Los Angeles Lakers
- ☐ Memphis Grizzlies
- ☐ Miami Heat
- ☐ Milwaukee Bucks
- ☐ Minnesota Timberwolves
- ☐ New Orleans Pelicans
- ☐ New York Knicks
- ☐ Oklahoma City Thunder
- ☐ Orlando Magic
- ☐ Philadelphia 76ers
- ☐ Phoenix Suns
- ☐ Portland Trail Blazers
- ☐ Sacramento Kings
- ☐ San Antonio Spurs
- ☐ Toronto Raptors
- ☐ Utah Jazz
- ☐ Washington Wizards

About the Author

Jake is a 13-year-old sports fan who loves football, American football, and basketball. He plays soccer as a goalie and dreams of one day playing for West Ham United and helping teach kids to love the game. His passion for sports runs in the family - his dad was a professional baseball player, and his stepdad sparked his love for West Ham. Through the Fun Fan Facts series, he shares the fun and excitement of sports with fans everywhere.

www.ingramcontent.com/pod-product-compliance
Lightning Source LLC
Chambersburg PA
CBHW050043040726
47599CB00015B/1783